TODDLER WORKBOOK

Fun and Educational Activity Book for Toddlers.

Teaches Letters, Shapes and Numbers.
Includes letter and number recognition, early math counting, days of the week, months of the year and large coloring activities.

Toddler Workbook

This workbook belongs to:

_____

Color the letter:

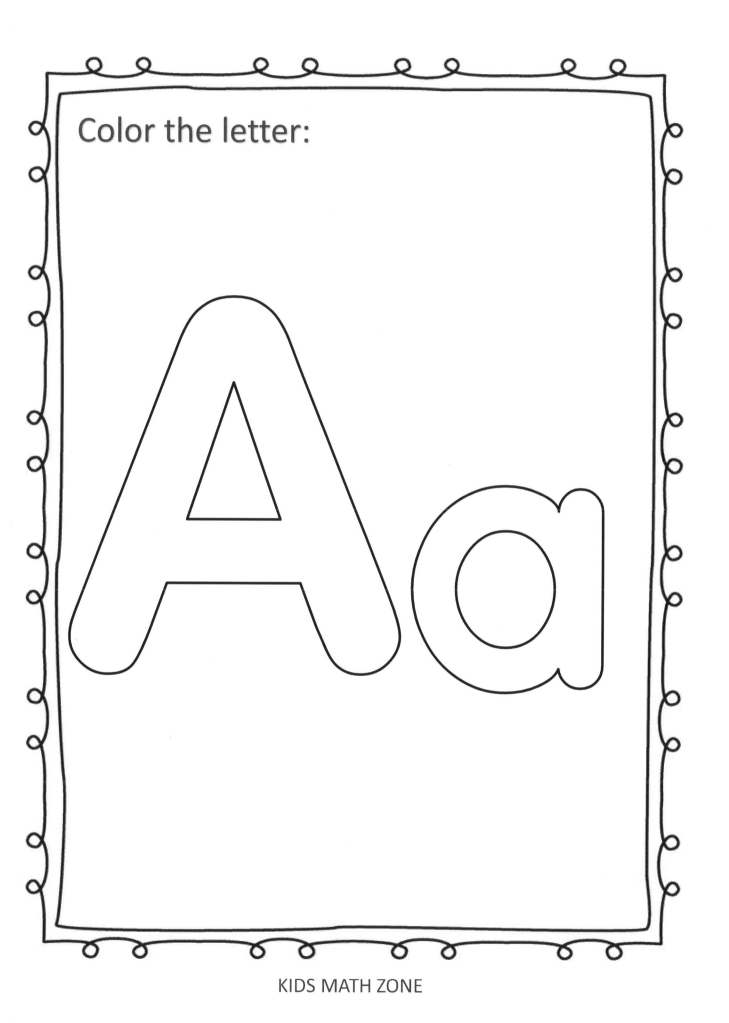

Color the letter:

Color the letter:

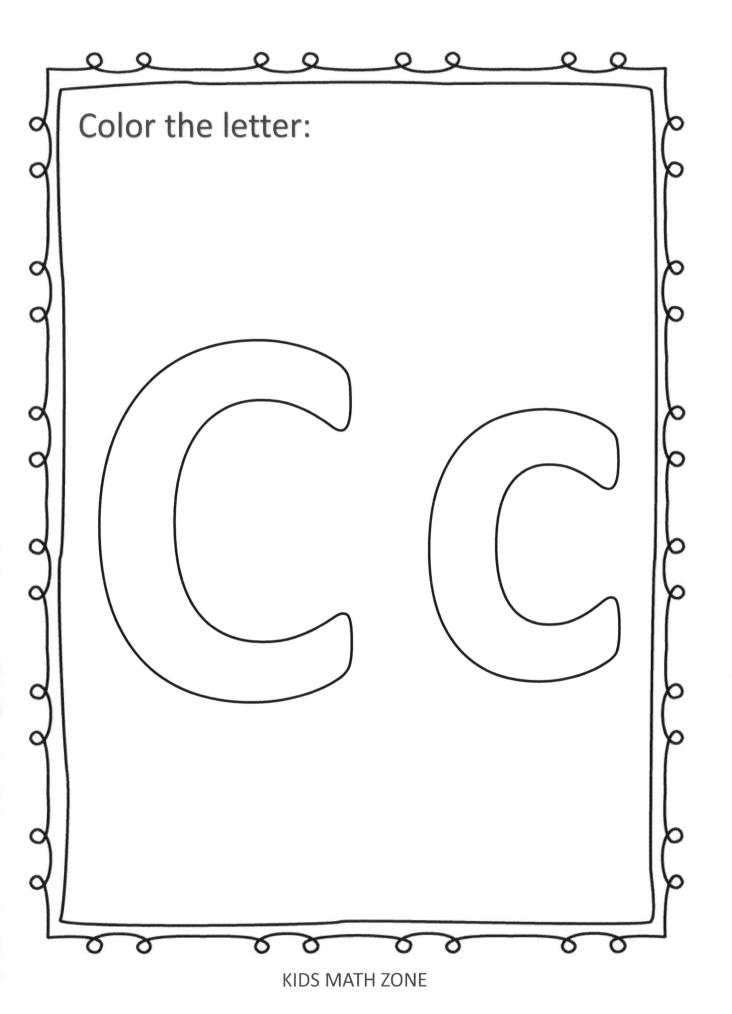

Color the letter:

Color the letter:

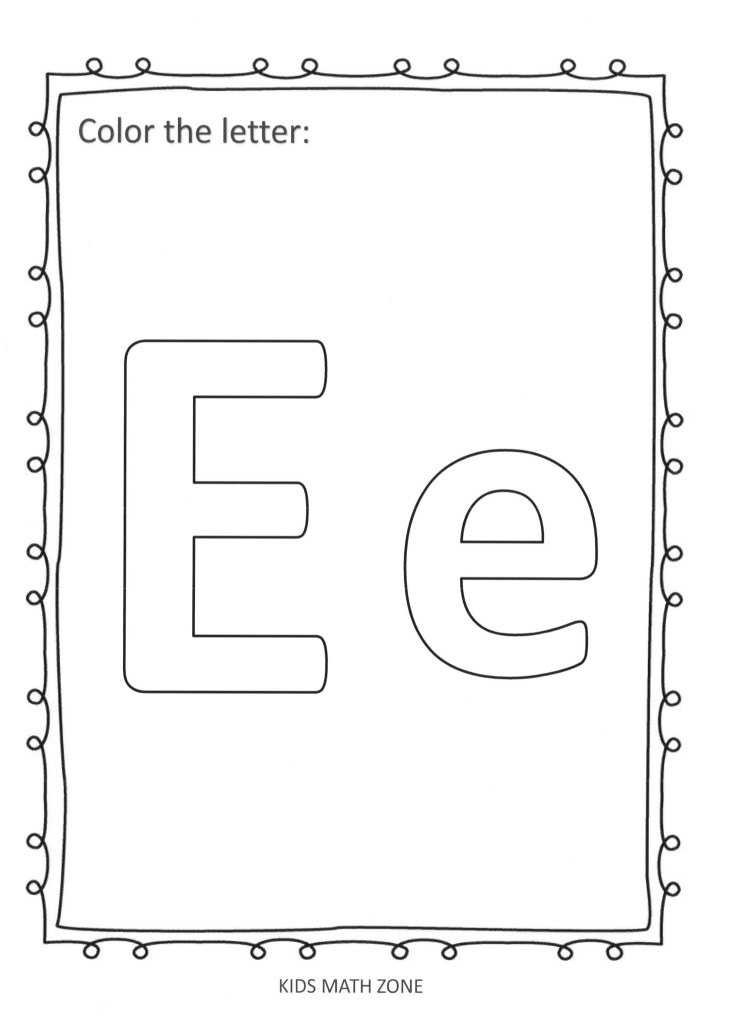

Color the letter:

Color the letter:

G g

Color the letter:

Color the letter:

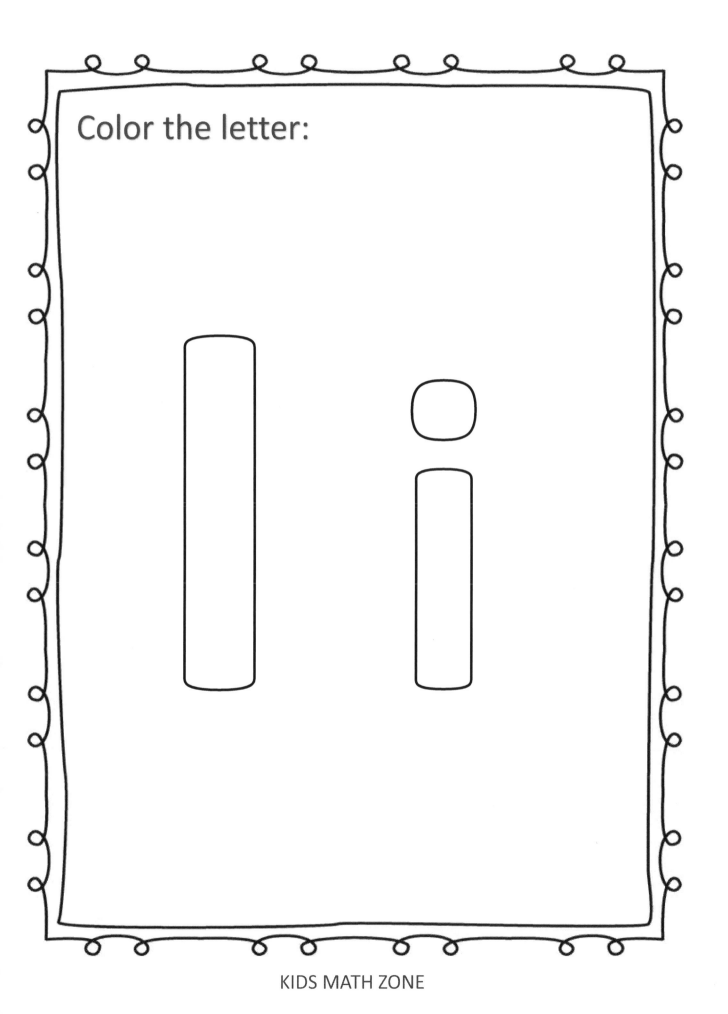

Color the letter:

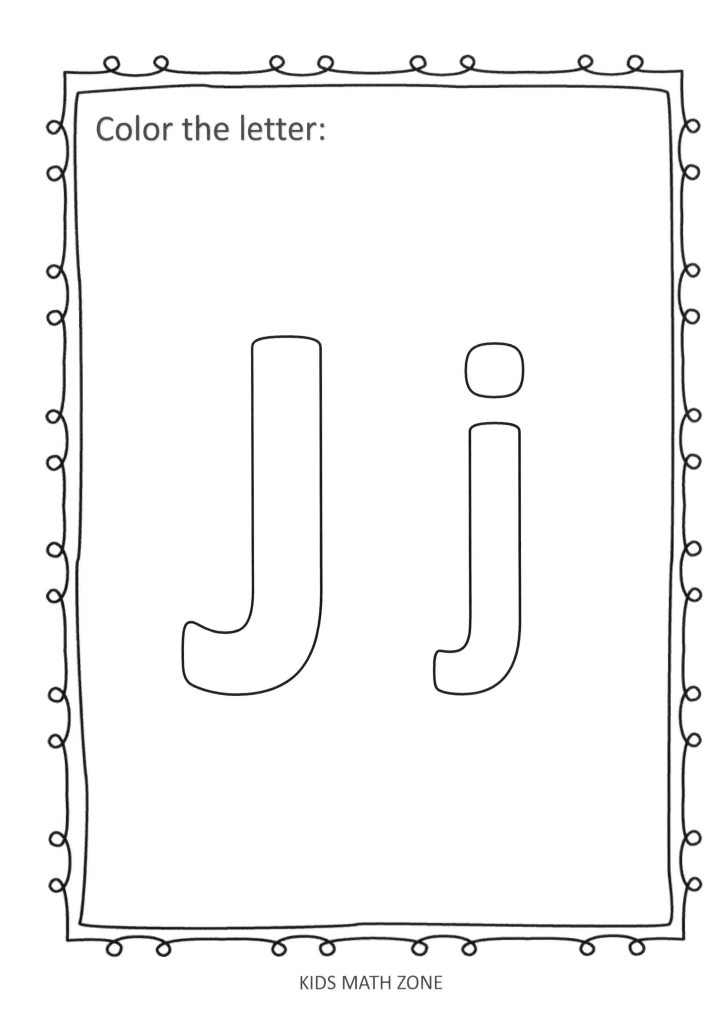

Color the letter:

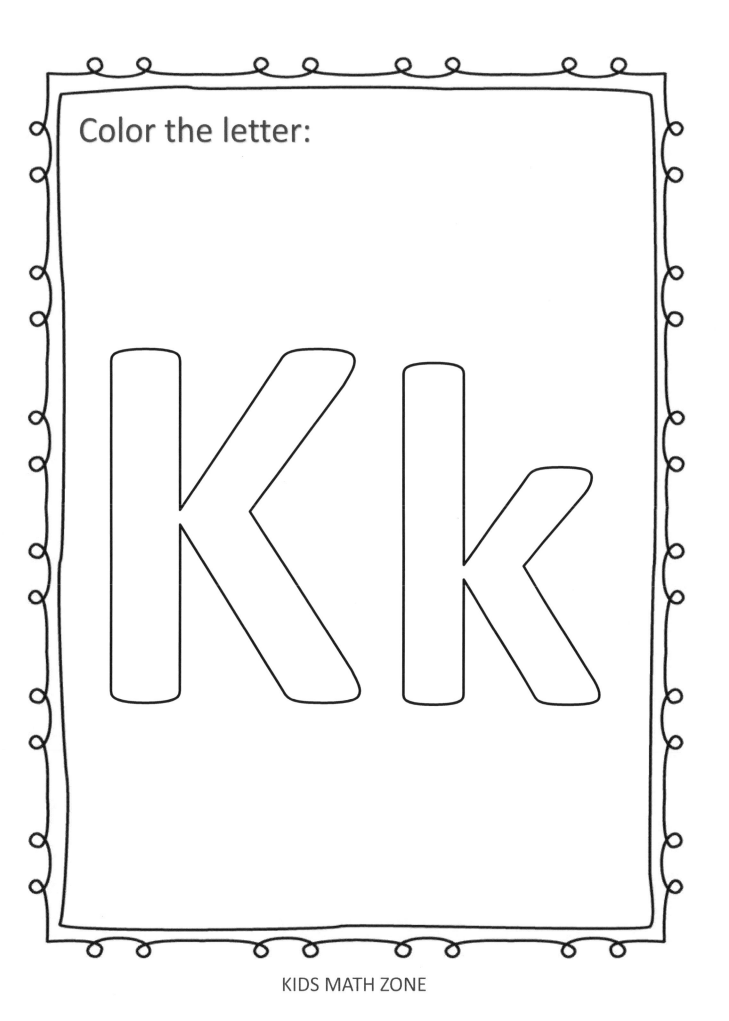

Color the letter:

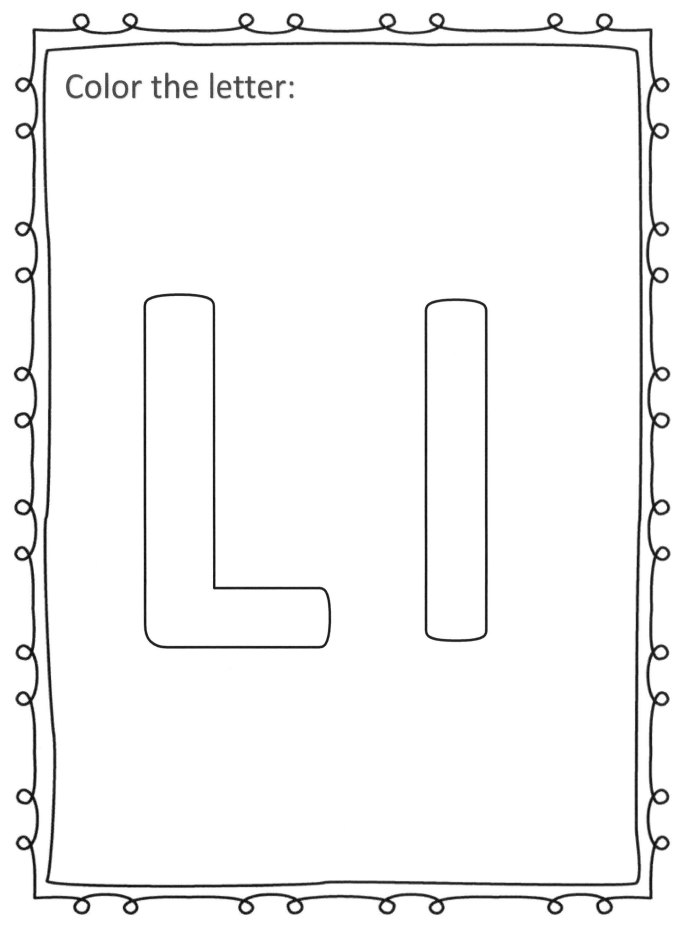

Color the letter:

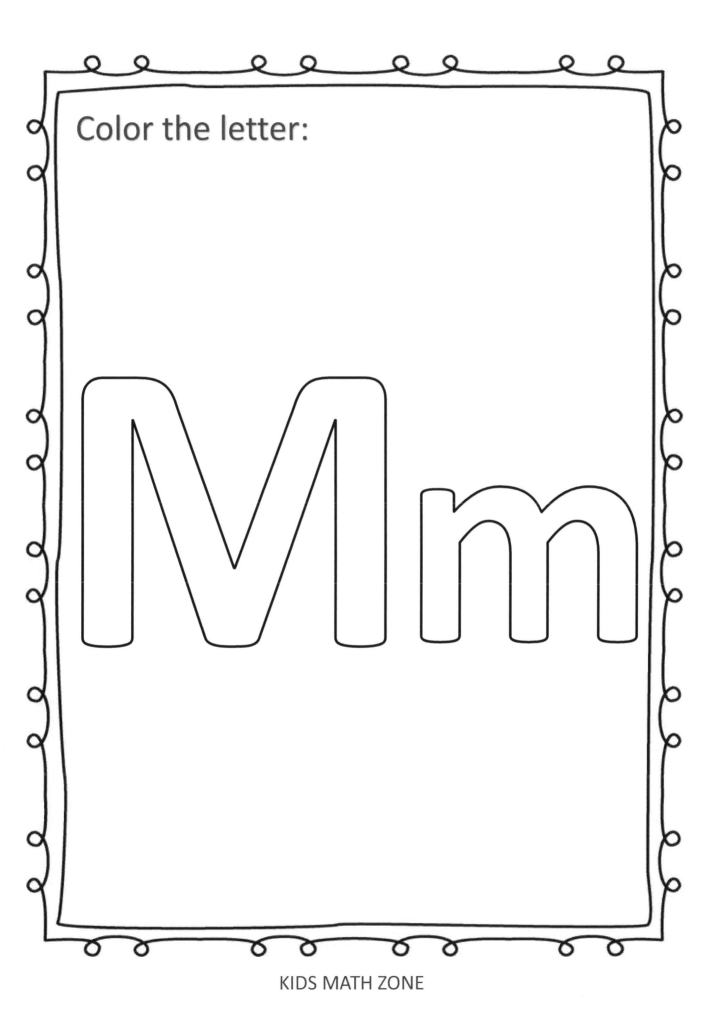

Color the letter:

Color the letter:

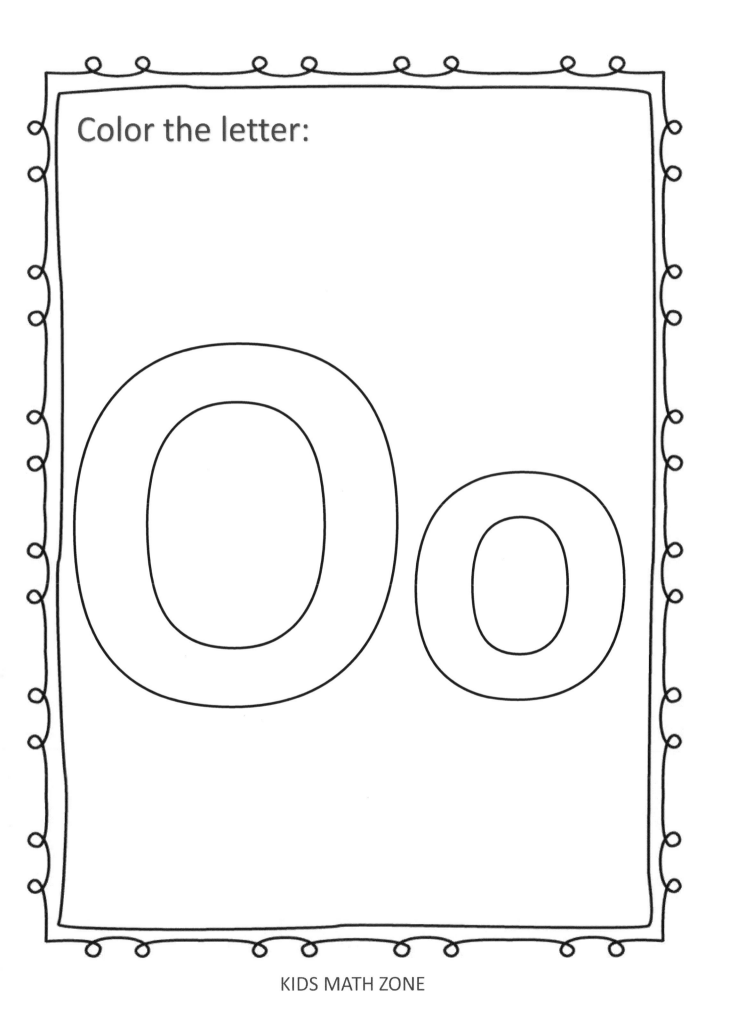

Color the letter:

Color the letter:

Color the letter:

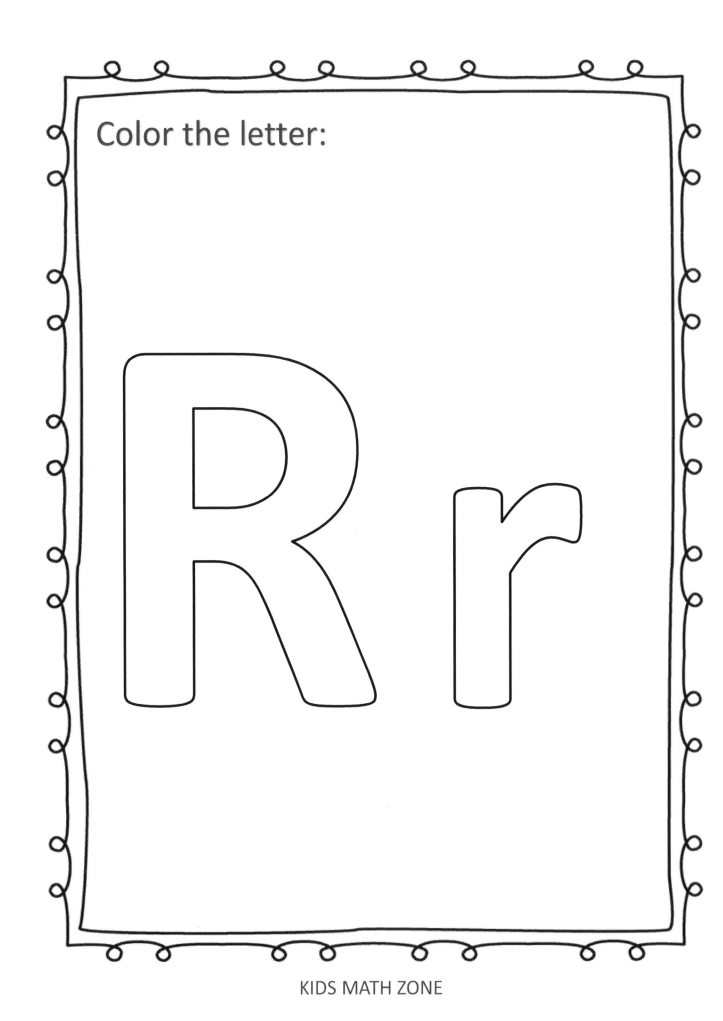

Color the letter:

Color the letter:

Color the letter:

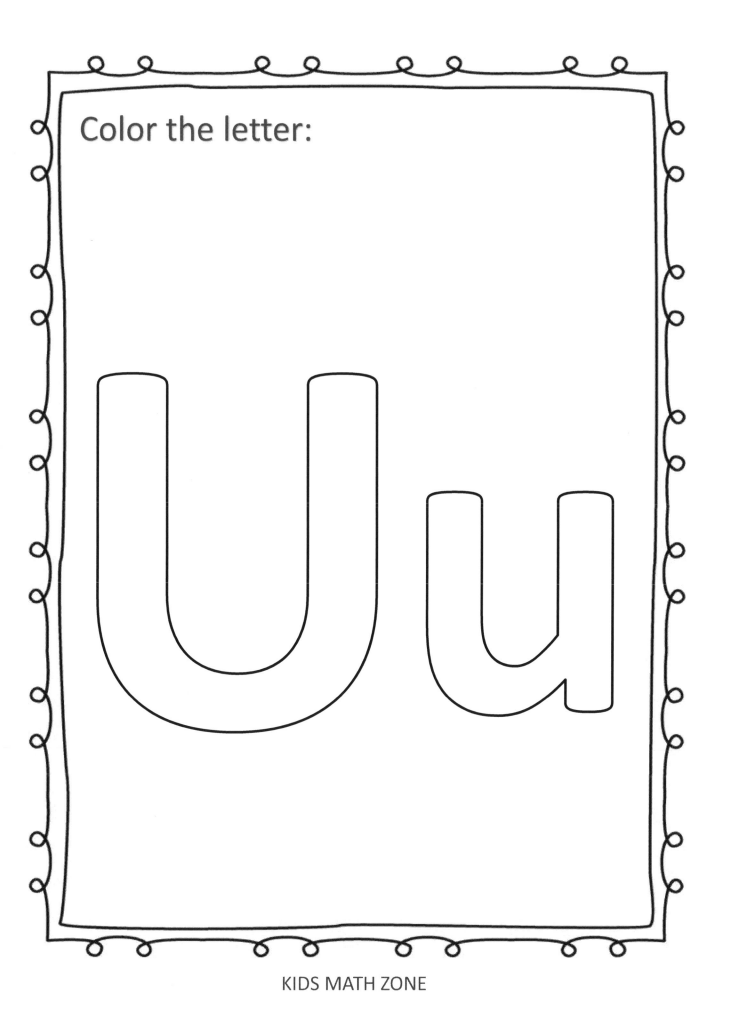

Color the letter:

Color the letter:

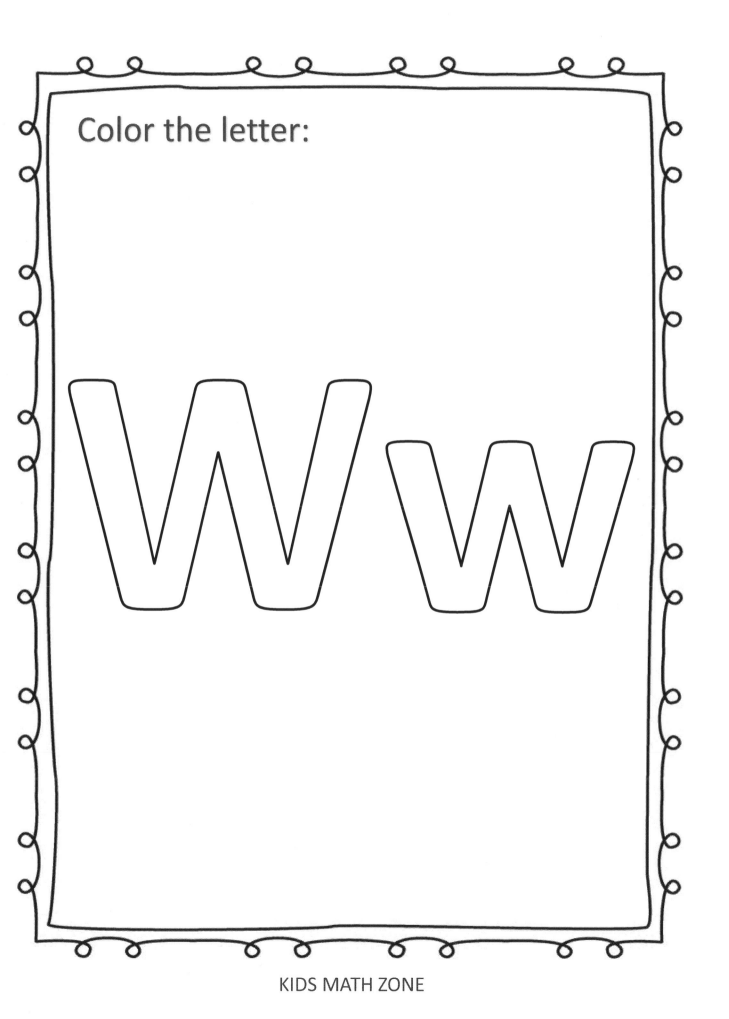

Color the letter:

Color the letter:

Color the letter:

ALPHABET LETTERS

A B C D E

F G H I J

K L M N O P

Q R S T U

V W X Y Z

ALPHABET LETTERS

Trace the letters:

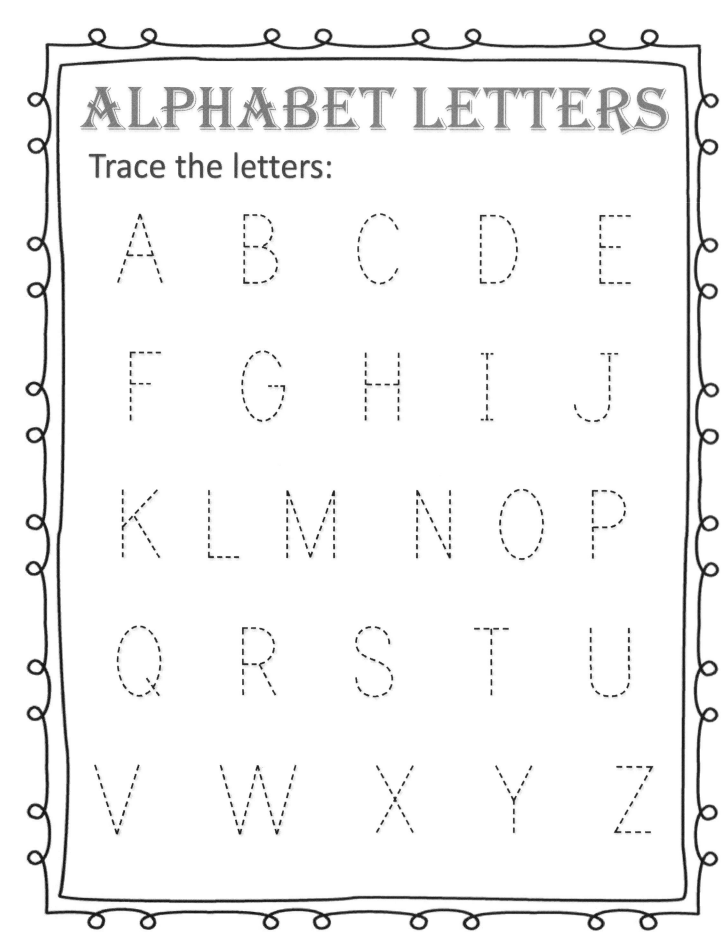

ALPHABET LETTERS

Trace the letters:

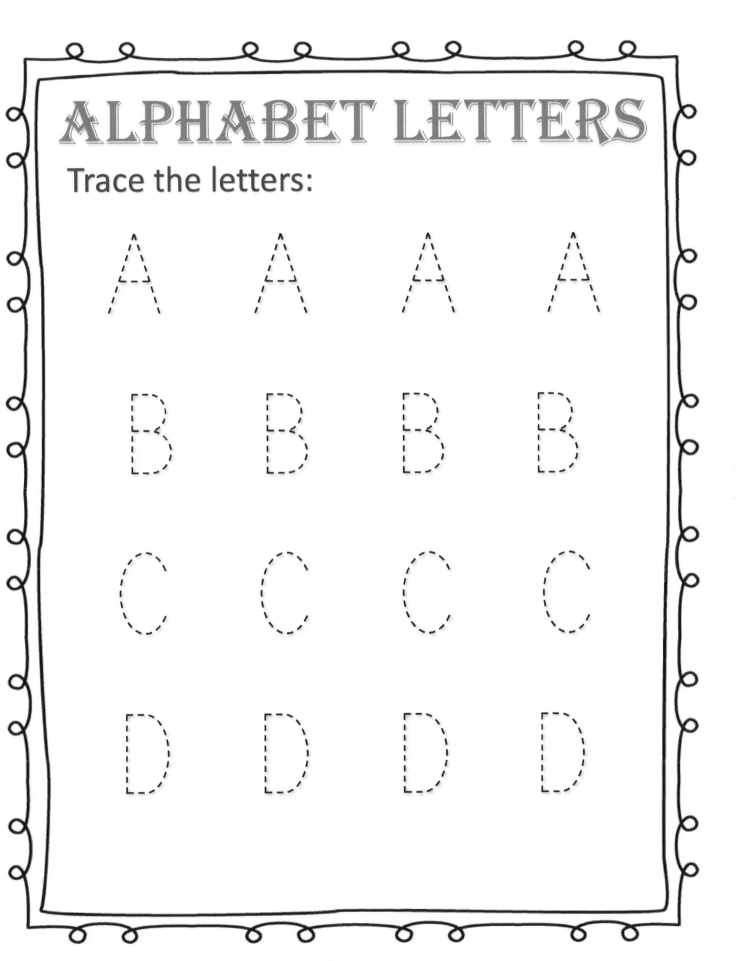

ALPHABET LETTERS

Trace the letters:

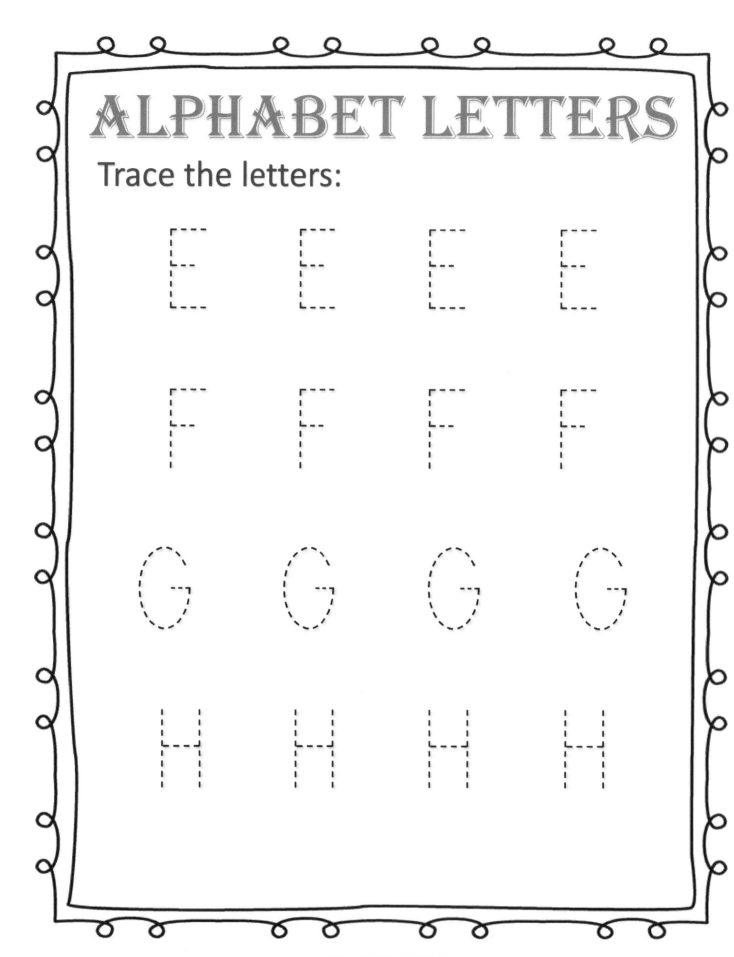

ALPHABET LETTERS

Trace the letters:

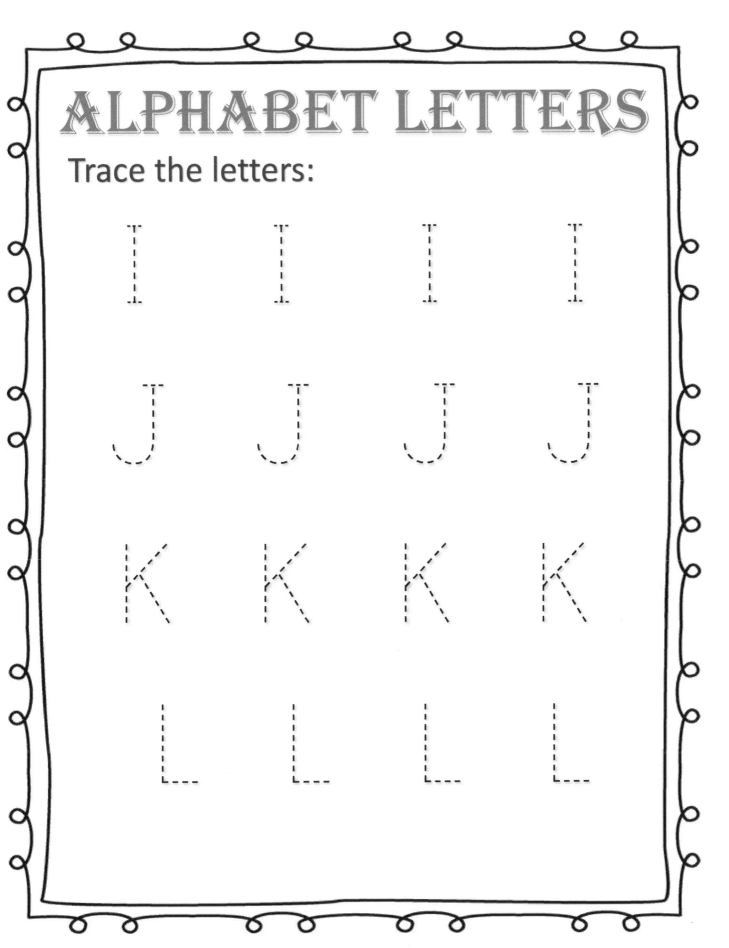

ALPHABET LETTERS

Trace the letters:

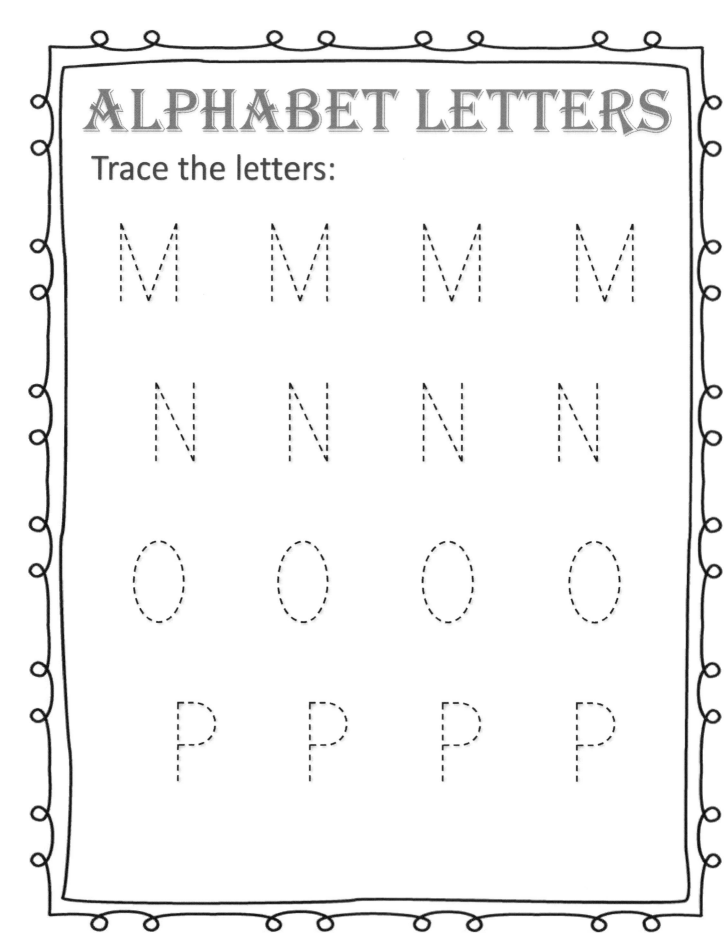

ALPHABET LETTERS

Trace the letters:

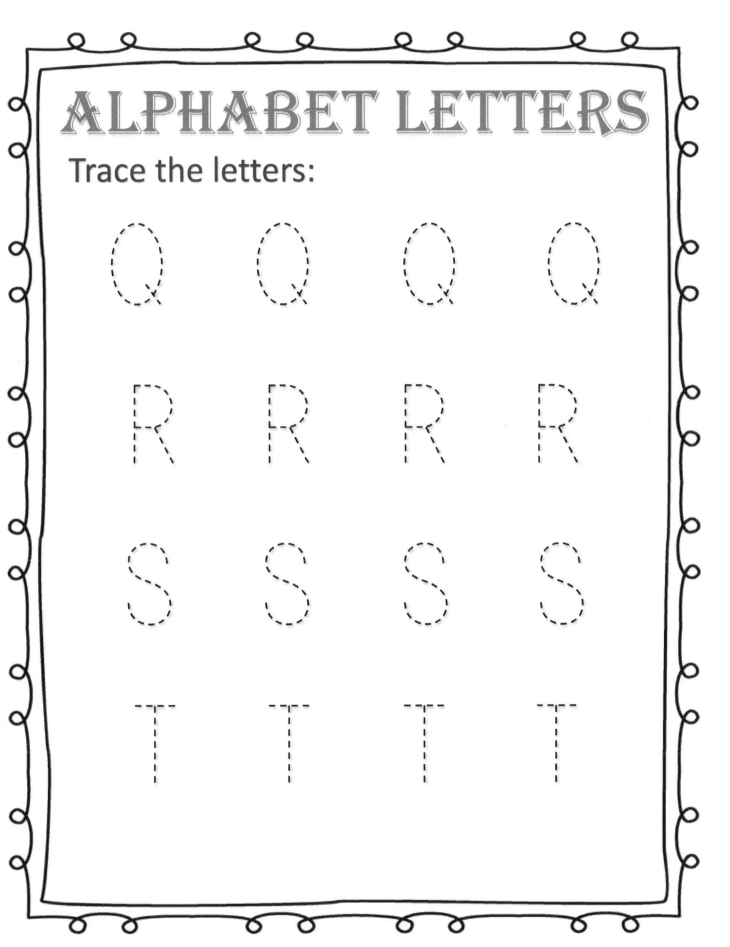

ALPHABET LETTERS

Trace the letters:

ALPHABET LETTERS

Trace the letters:

SHAPES

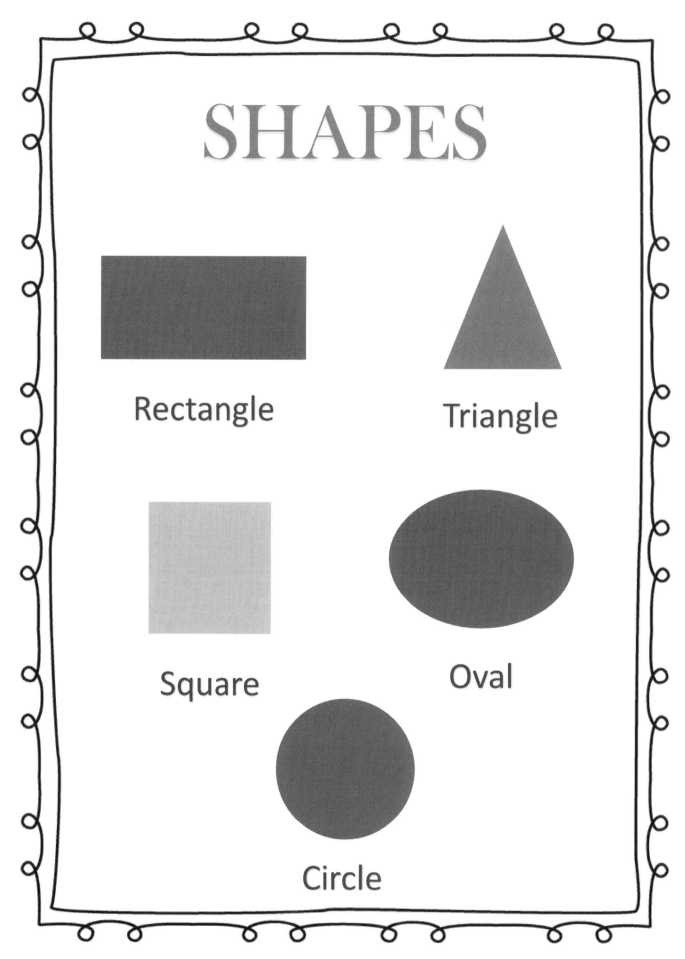

Rectangle

Triangle

Square

Oval

Circle

SHAPES

Trace the shapes:

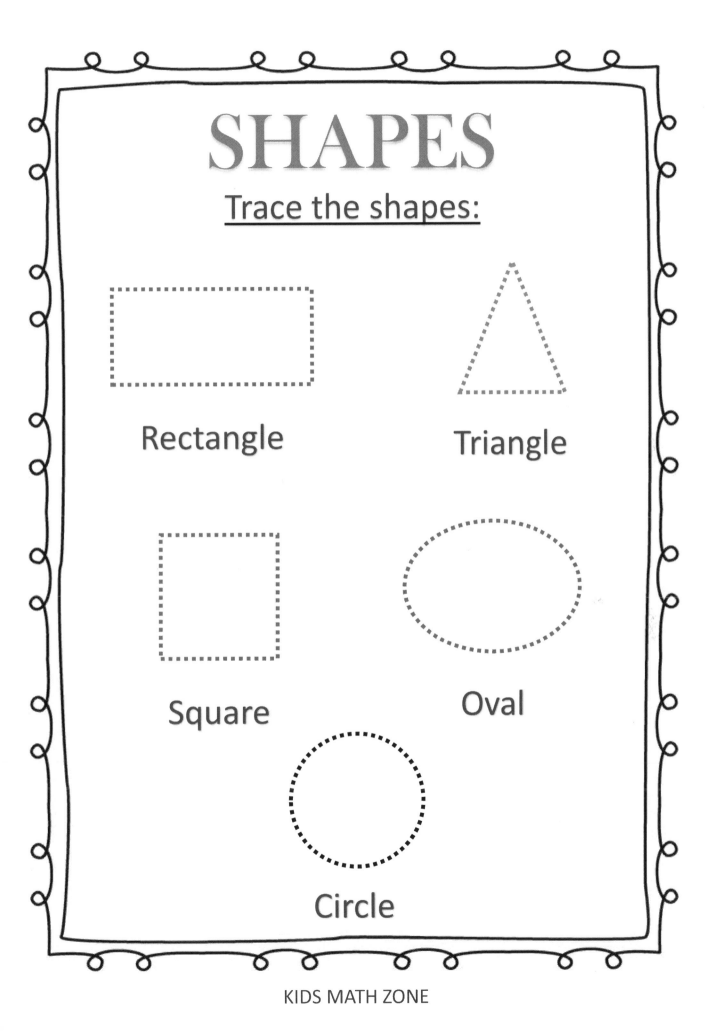

Rectangle

Triangle

Square

Oval

Circle

OVAL

Trace each oval:

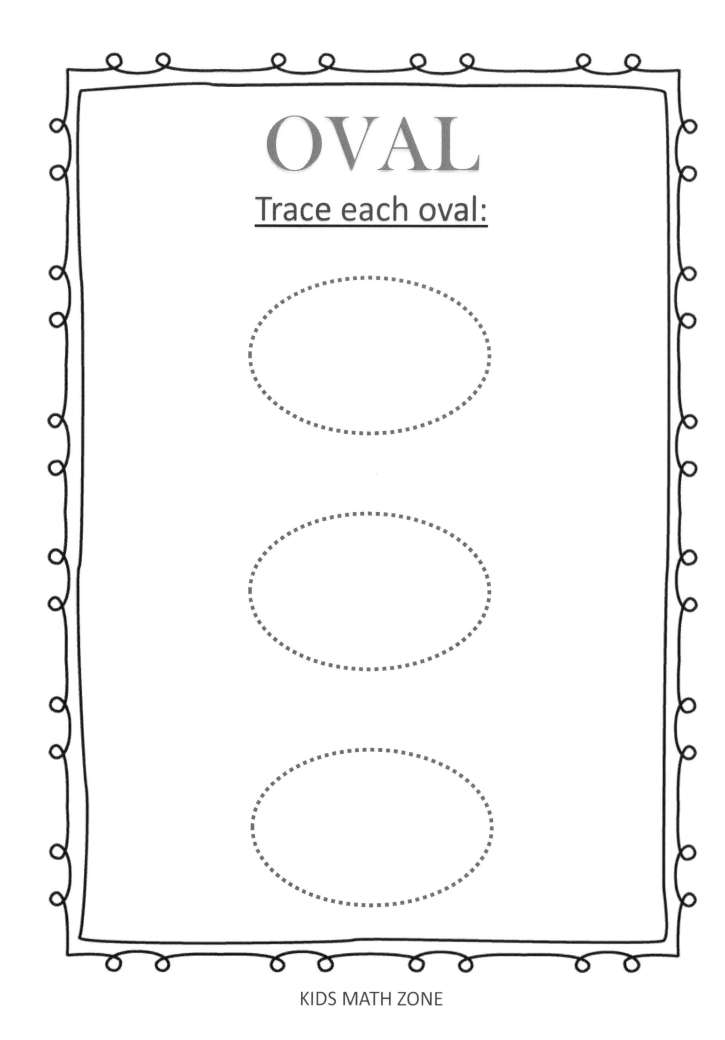

SQUARE

Trace each square:

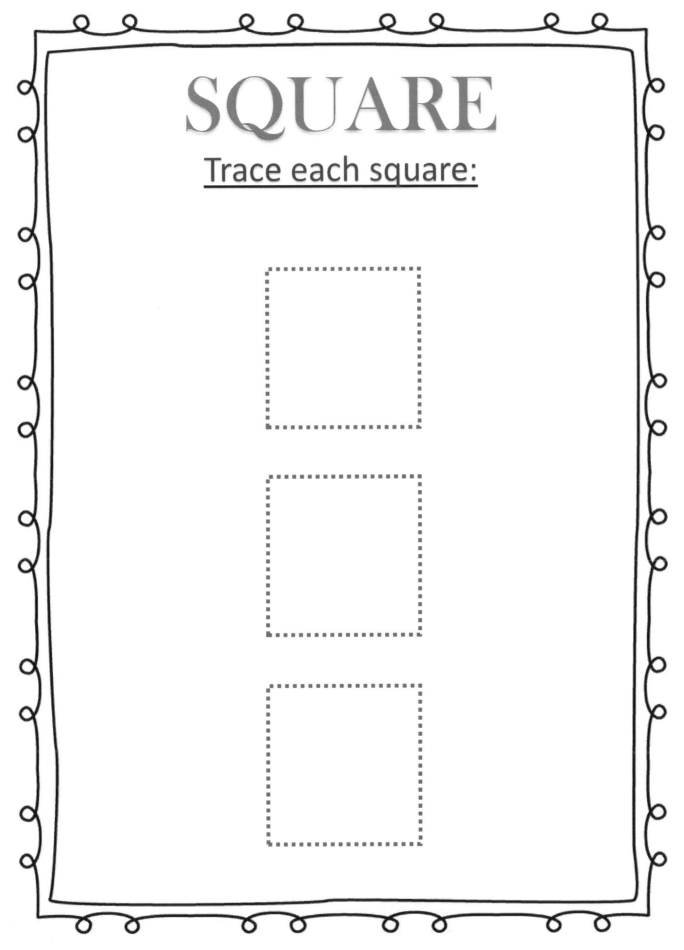

RECTANGLE

Trace each rectangle:

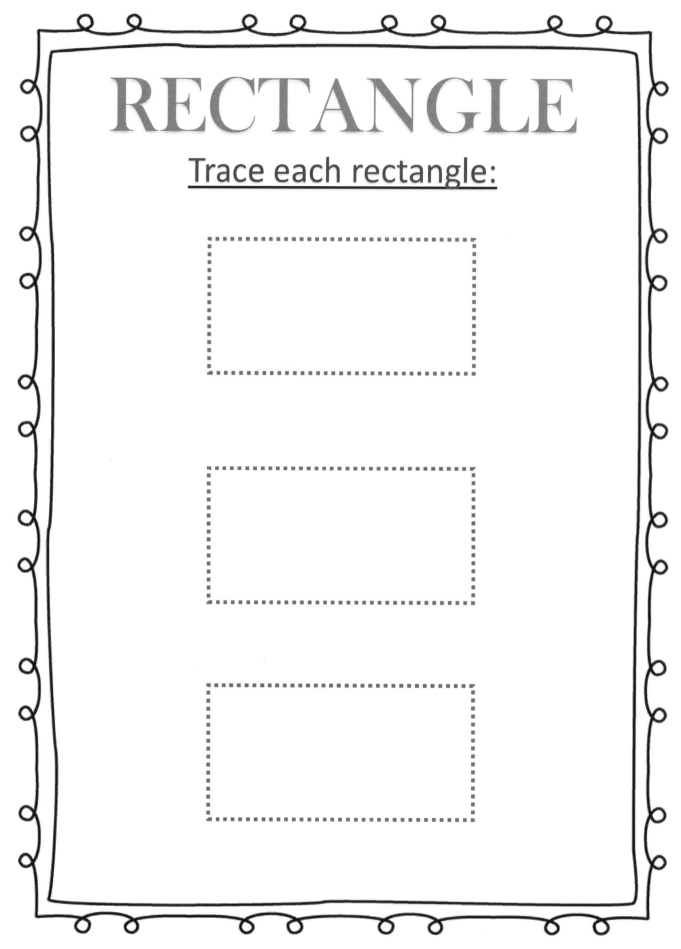

CIRCLE

Trace each circle:

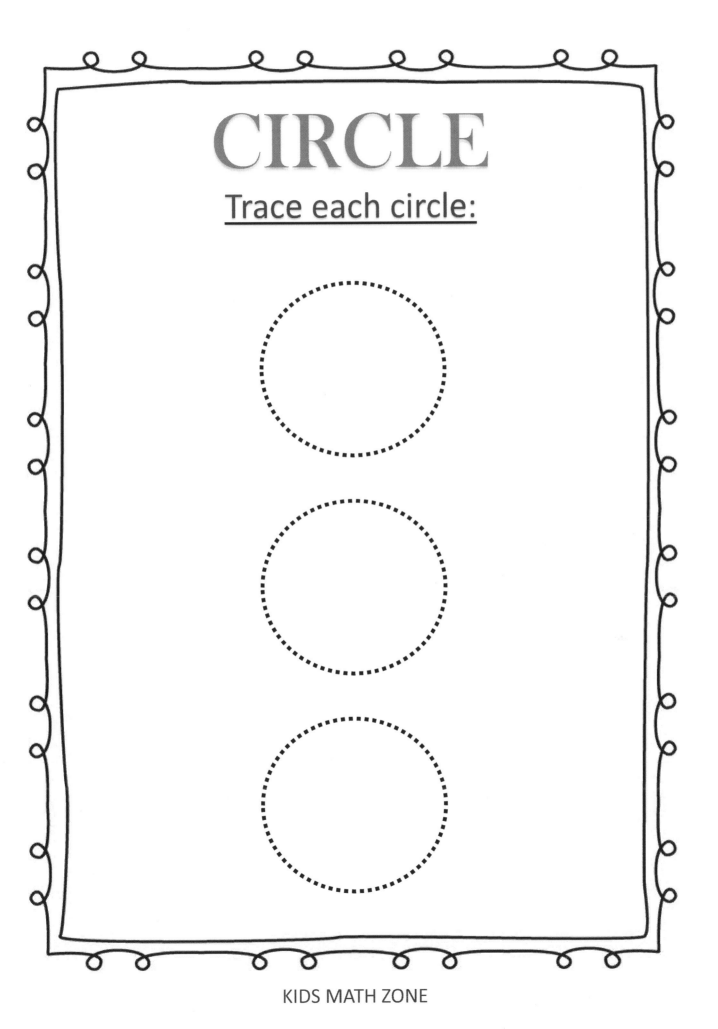

TRIANGLE

Trace each triangle:

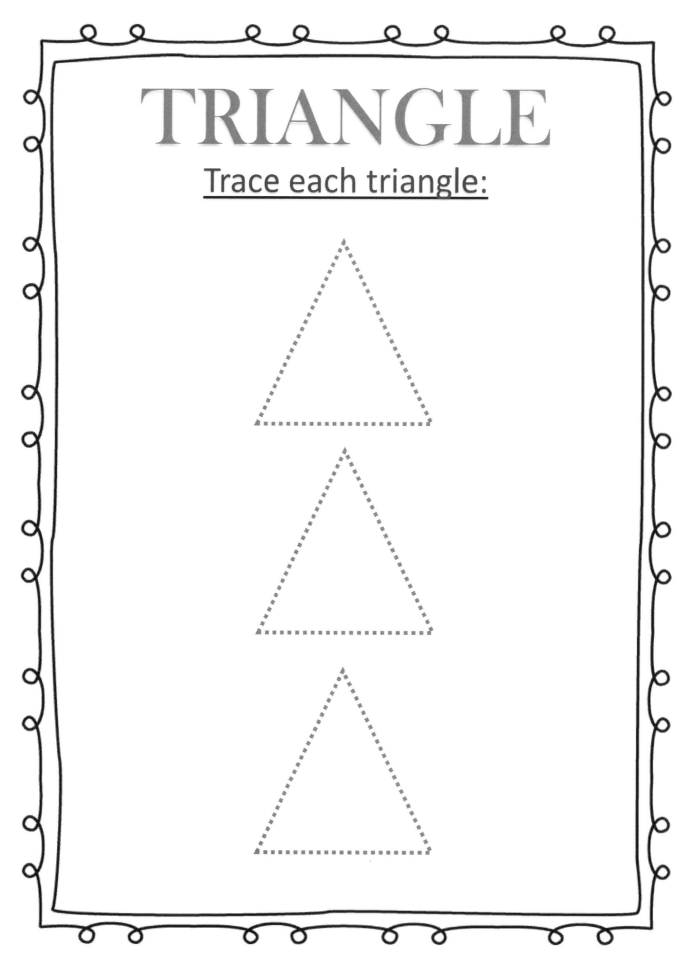

SHAPES

Color the circles

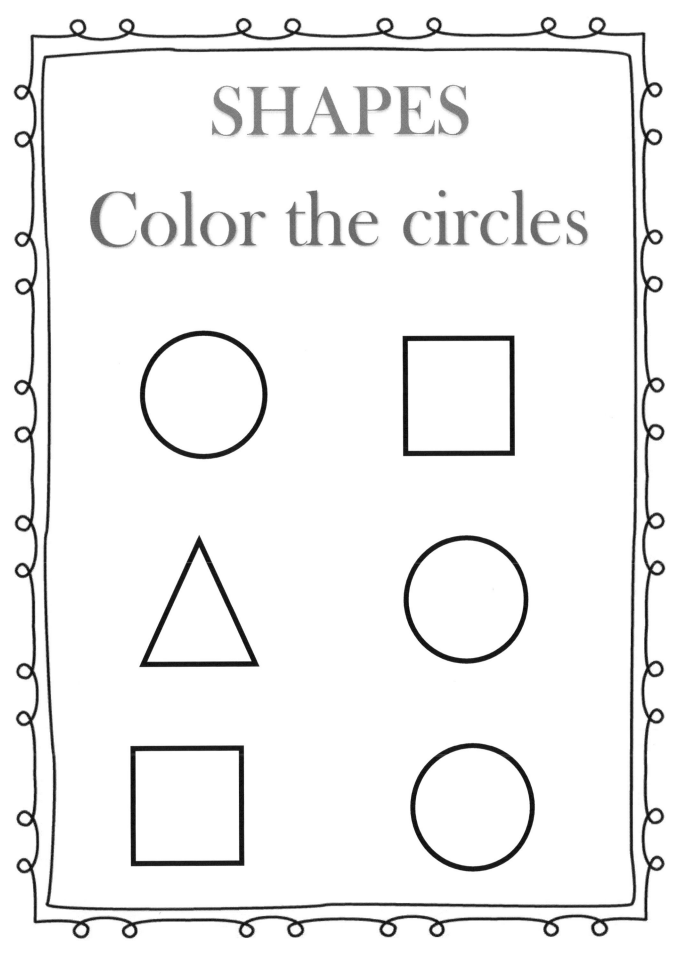

SHAPES

Color the squares

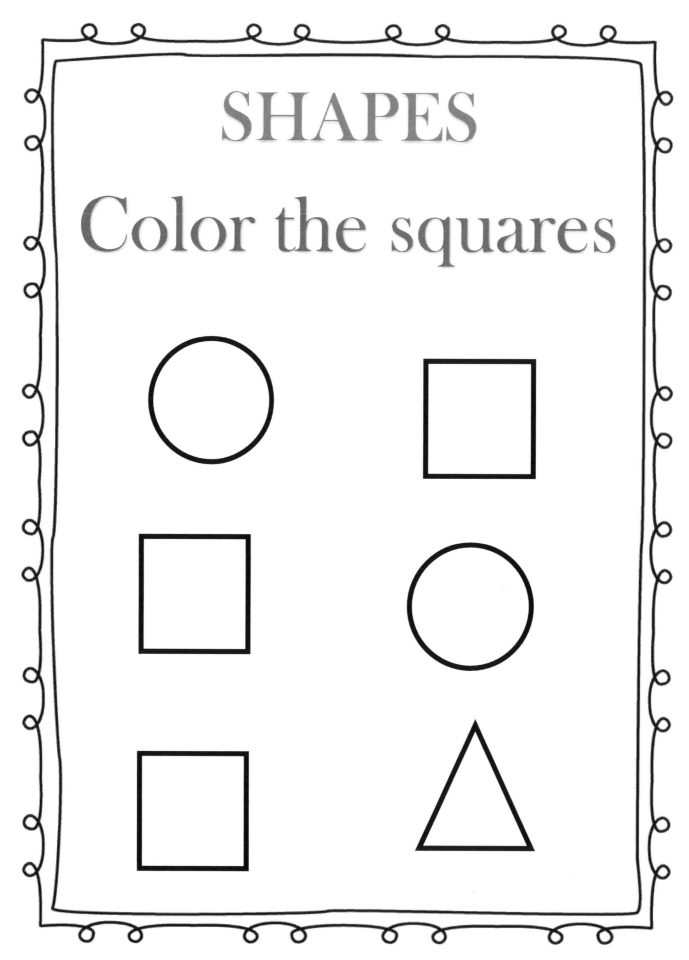

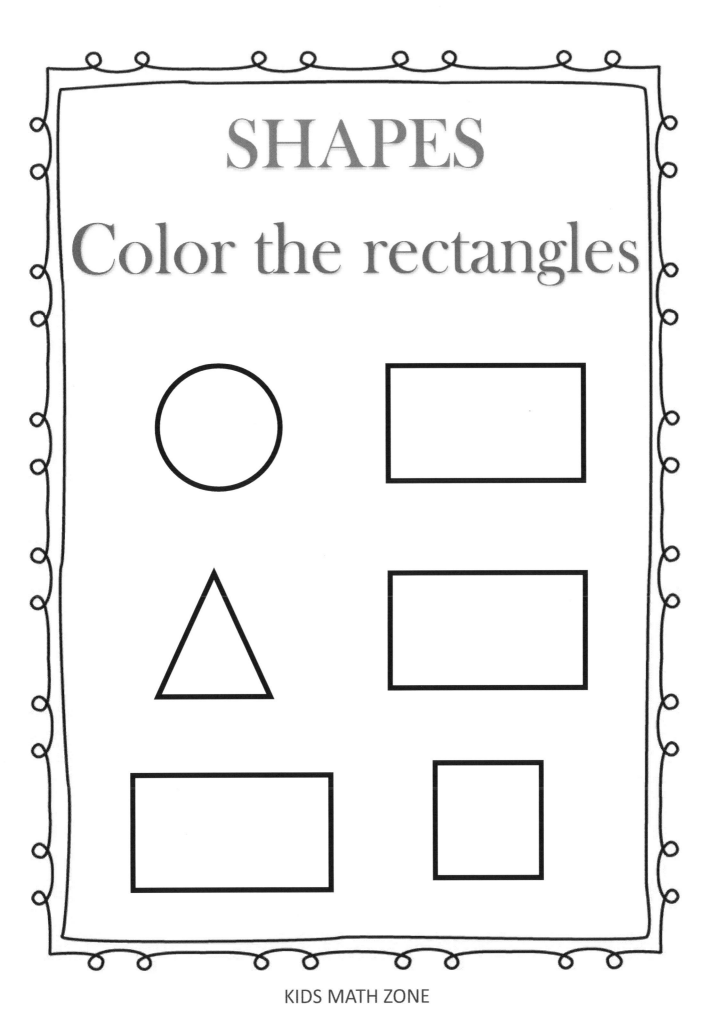

SHAPES

Color the rectangles

SHAPES

Color the triangles

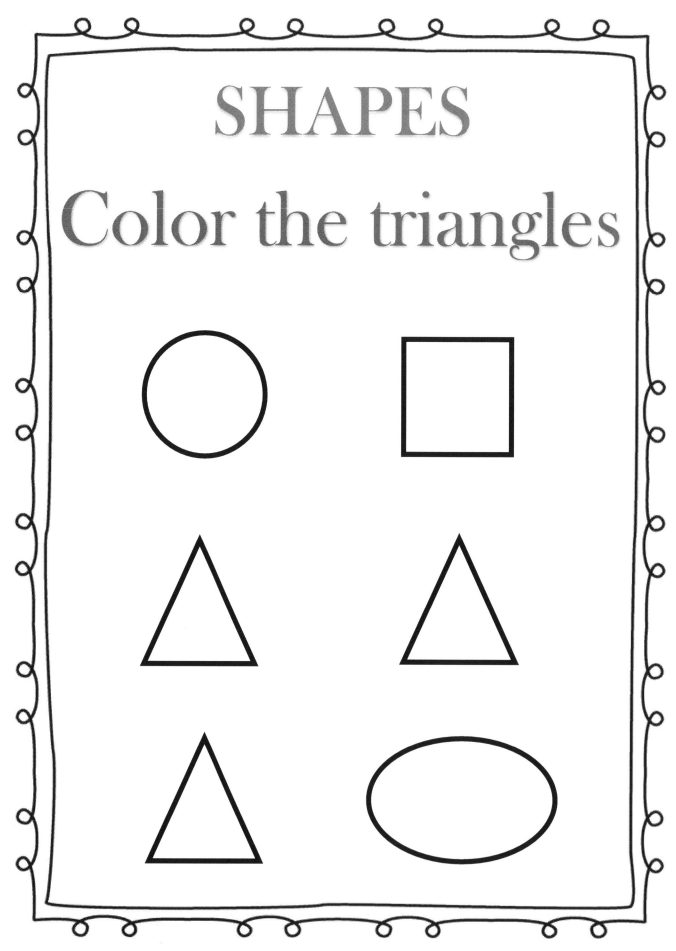

SHAPES

Color the ovals

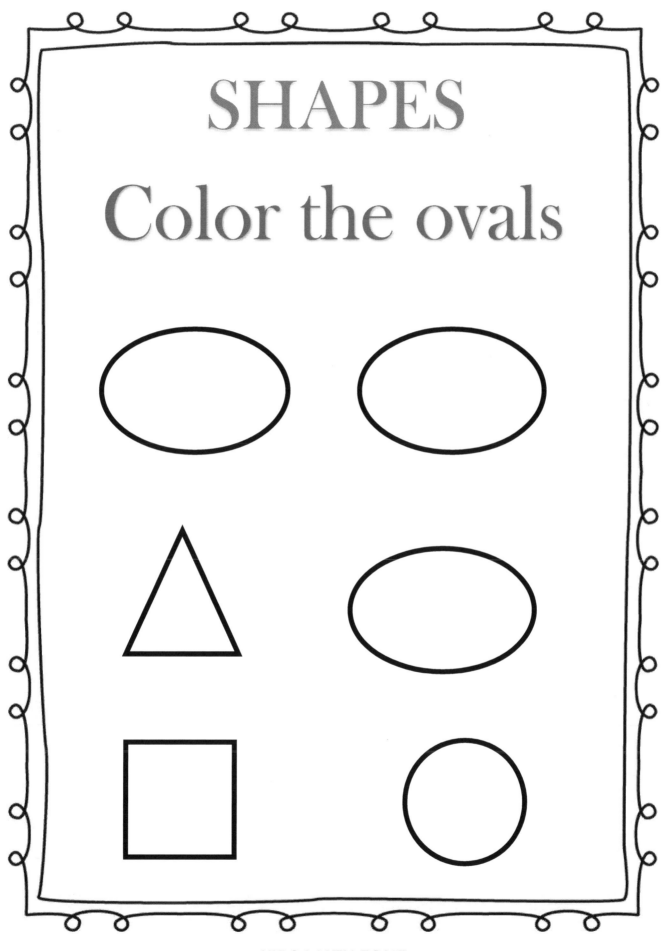

SHAPES

Connect the same shapes:

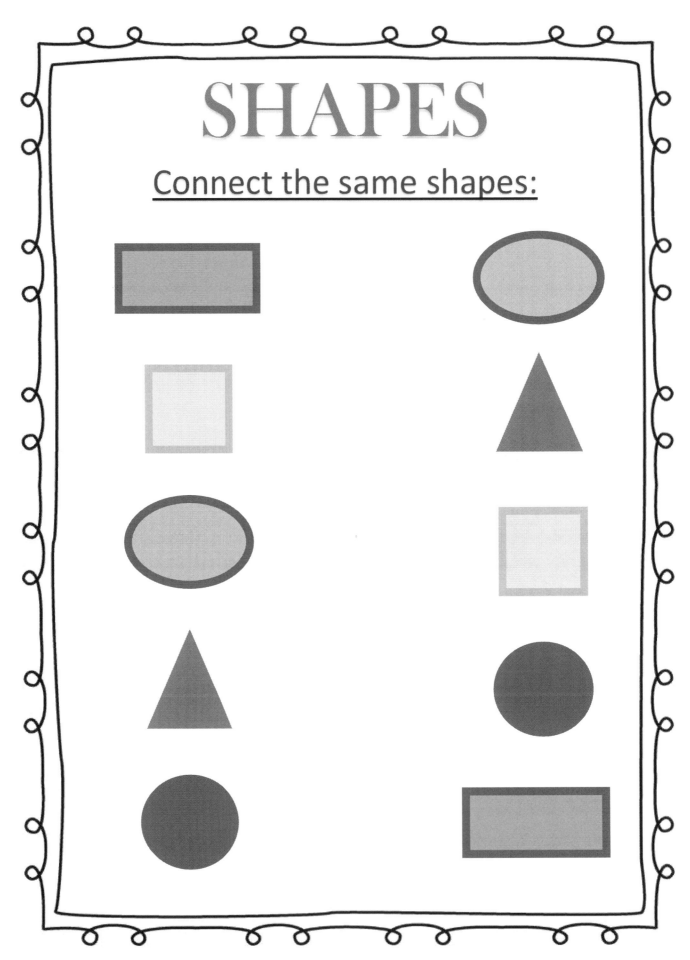

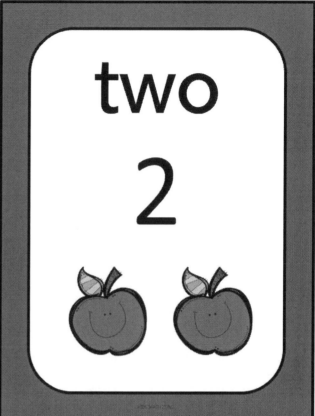

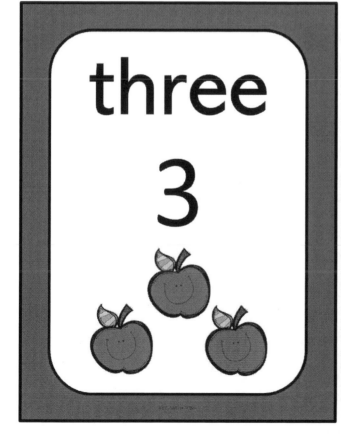

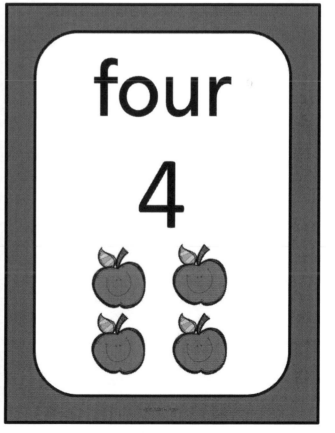

This page intentionally left blank for flash cards to be cut out.

five
5

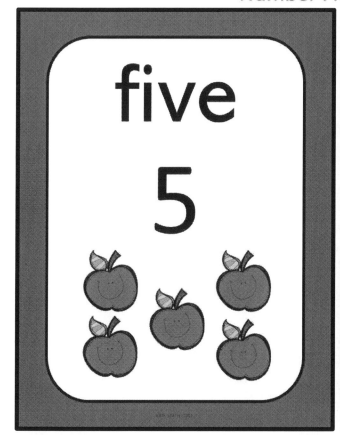

six
6

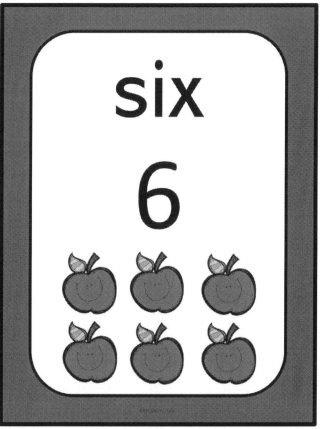

seven
7

eight
8

This page intentionally left blank for flash cards to be cut out.

nine
9

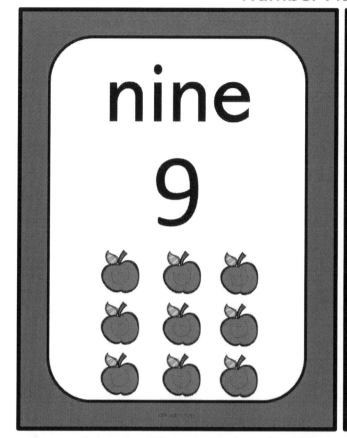

ten
10

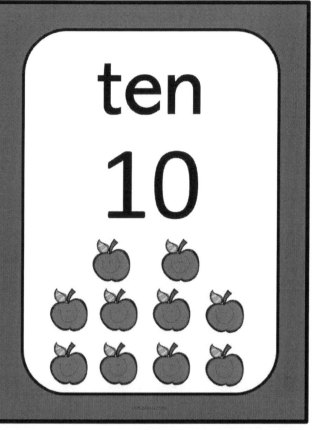

eleven
11

twelve
12

This page intentionally left blank for flash cards to be cut out.

thirteen
13

fourteen
14

fifteen
15

sixteen
16

This page intentionally left blank for flash cards to be cut out.

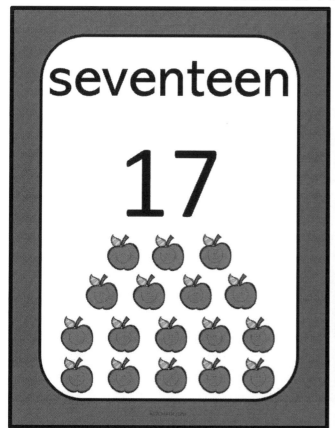

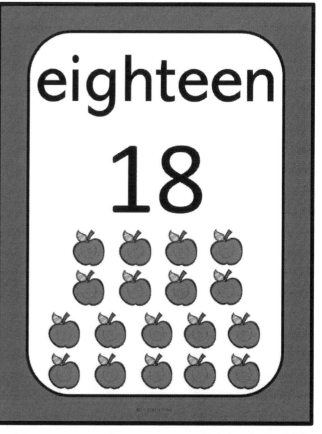

seventeen 17

eighteen 18

nineteen 19

twenty 20

This page intentionally left blank for flash cards to be cut out.

NUMBERS

1 2 3 4

5 6 7 8

9 10 11 12

13 14 15 16

17 18 19 20

NUMBERS

Trace the Numbers

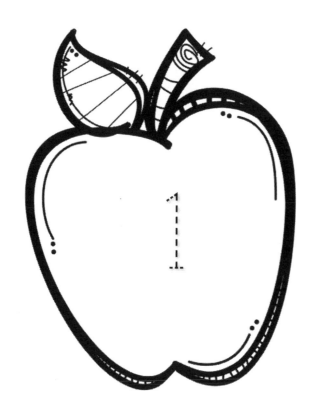

Trace the Numbers

2 2 2 2 2

Trace the Numbers

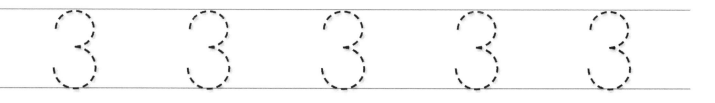

Trace the Numbers

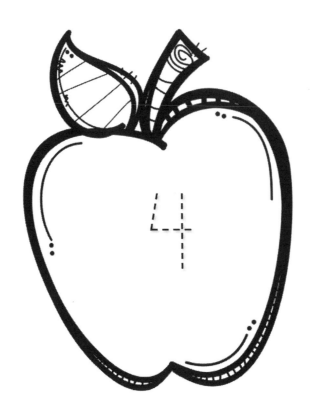

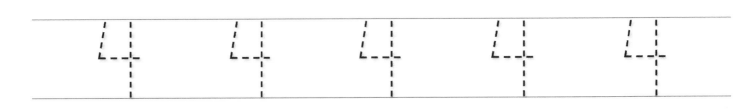

Trace the Numbers

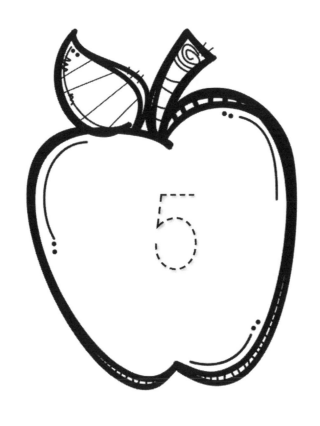

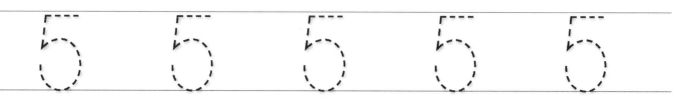

Trace the Numbers

6   6   6   6   6

Trace the Numbers

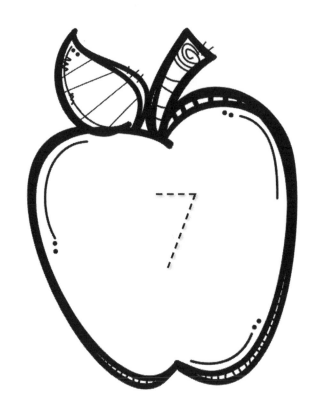

7 7 7 7 7

Trace the Numbers

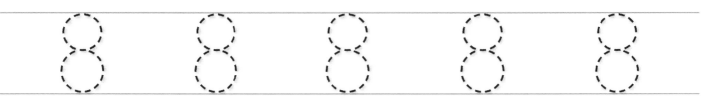

Trace the Numbers

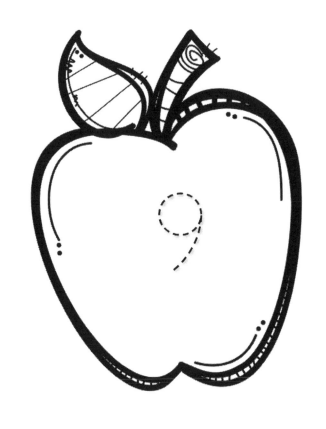

9 9 9 9 9

Trace the Numbers

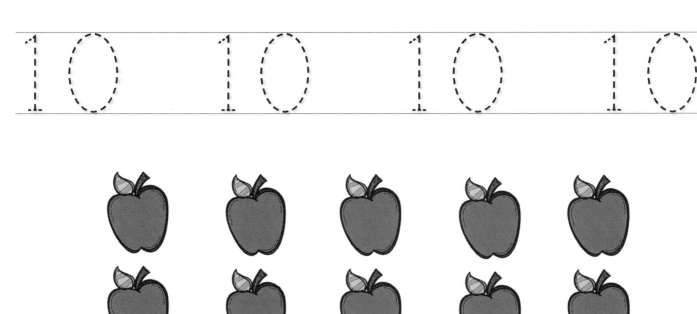

Trace the Numbers

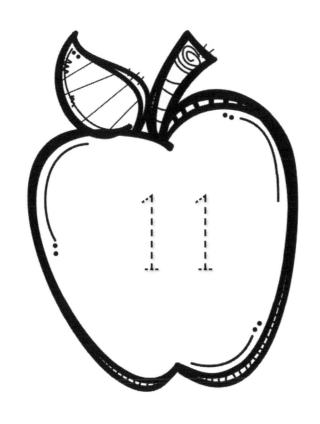

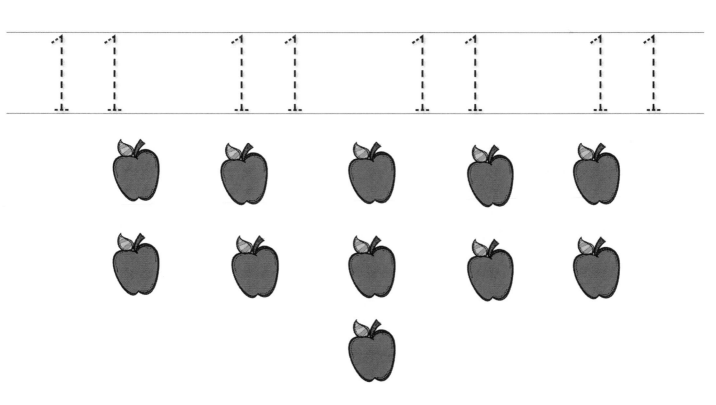

Trace the Numbers

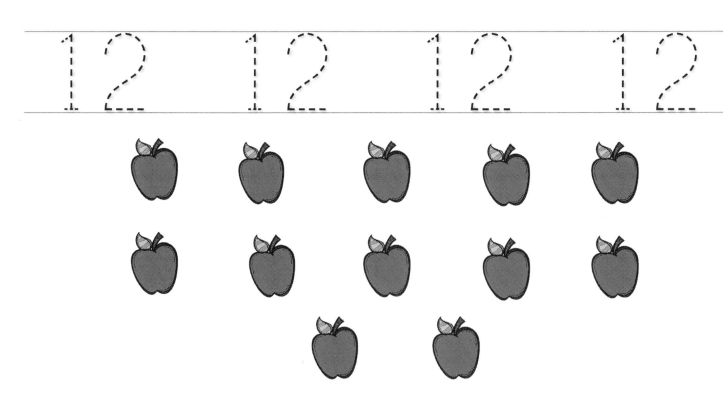

Trace the Numbers

13 13 13 13

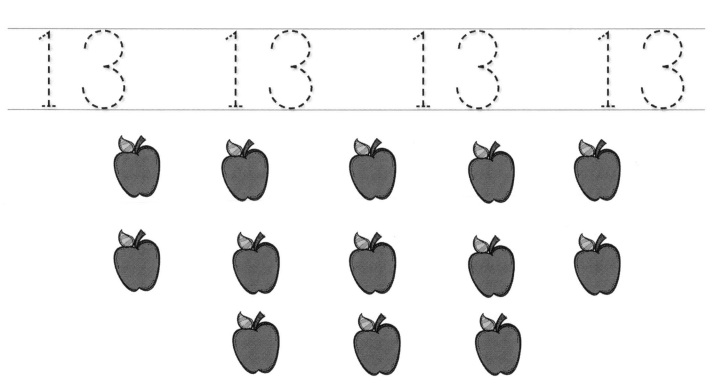

Trace the Numbers

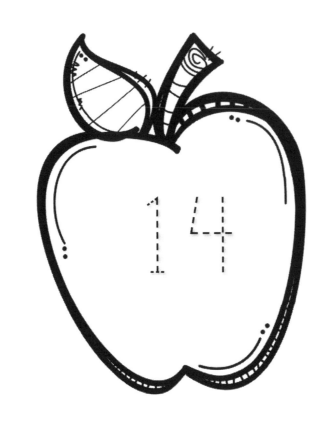

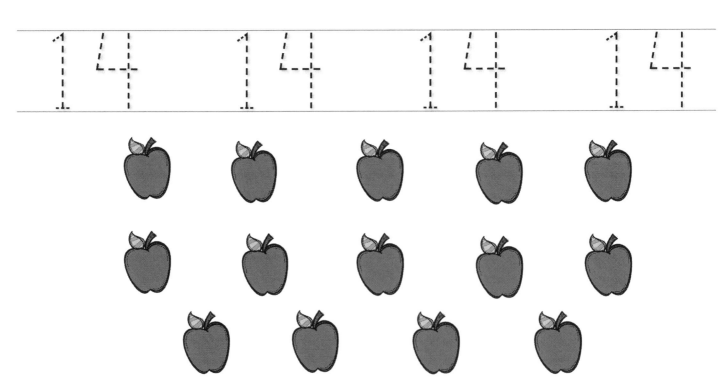

Trace the Numbers

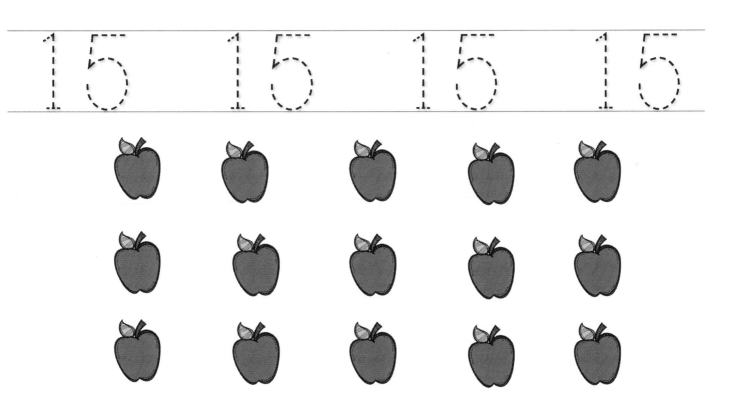

Trace the Numbers

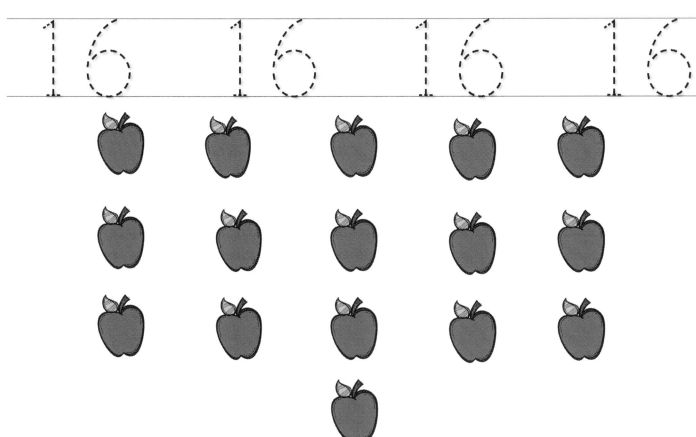

Trace the Numbers

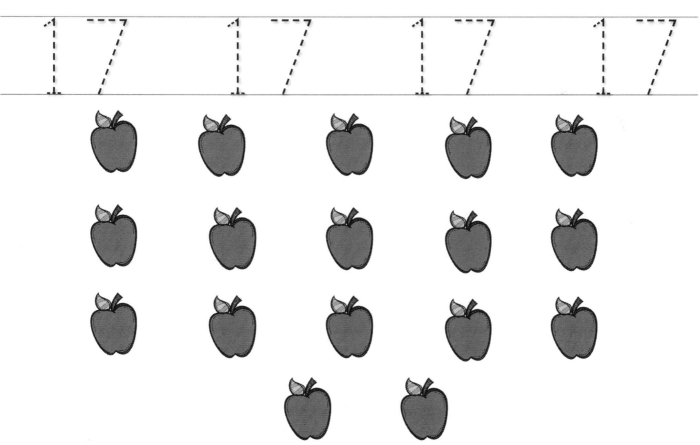

Trace the Numbers

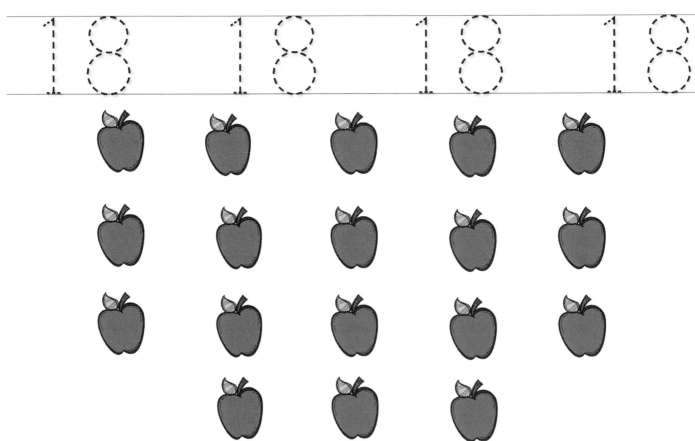

Trace the Numbers

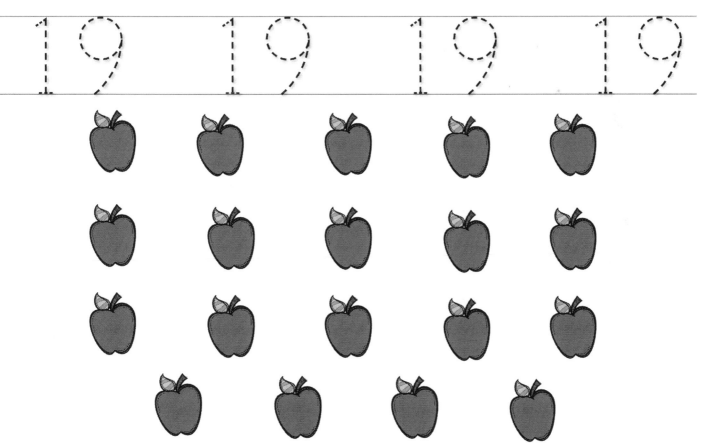

Trace the Numbers

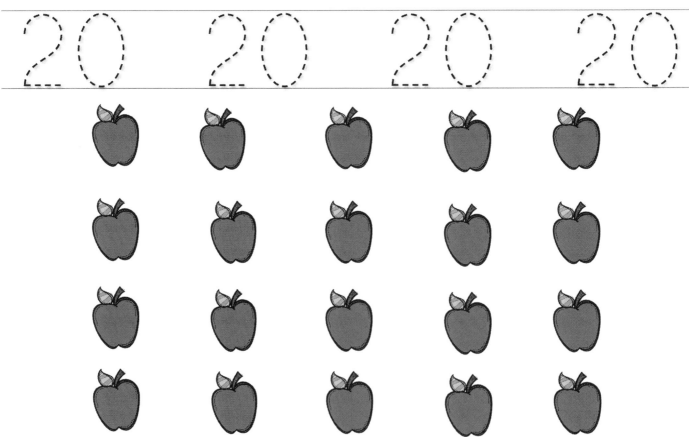

HOW MANY CAN YOU COUNT

Name: _____

How many flowers do you count below? Circle the correct number:

6   5   4

HOW MANY CAN YOU COUNT

Name: _____

How many flowers do you count below? Circle the correct number:

6	5	2

HOW MANY CAN YOU COUNT

Name: _____

How many apples do you count below? Circle the correct number:

7   6   10

HOW MANY CAN YOU COUNT

Name: _____

How many apples do you count below? Circle the correct number:

3	8	7

Count and MATCH

Count and match to correct number:

4

5

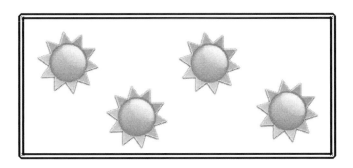
2

3

Count and MATCH

Count and match to correct number:

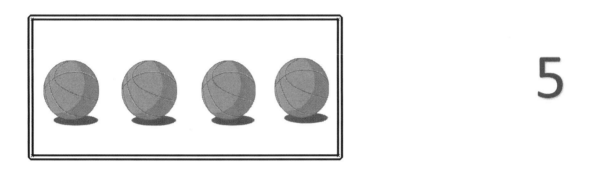

5

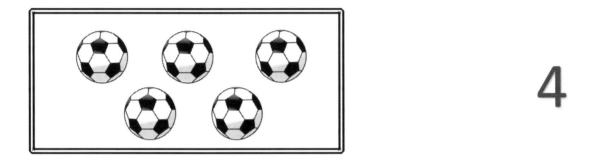

4

3

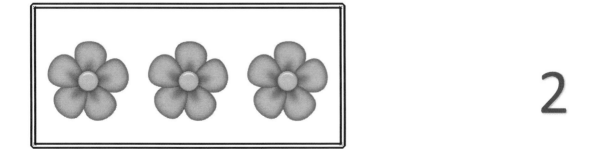

2

Connect the same ones:

Connect the same ones:

DAYS OF THE WEEK

SUNDAY

MONDAY

TUESDAY

WEDNESDAY

THURSDAY

FRIDAY

SATURDAY

MONTHS OF THE YEAR

JANUARY

FEBRUARY

MARCH

APRIL

MAY

JUNE

MONTHS OF THE YEAR

JULY

AUGUST

SEPTEMBER

OCTOBER

NOVEMBER

DECEMBER

Made in United States
Orlando, FL
08 June 2023

33933511R00052